Jose Antonio Ponce

Jose Antonio Ponce

Modern Catholic Prayers

By
Jose Antonio Ponce

Copyright 2021 by Jose Antonio Ponce.

All rights reserved. No part of this publication may be reproduced, distributed, or transmitted in any form or by any means, or stored in a database or retrieval system, without the prior written permission of the author except in the case of brief quotations embodied in critical articles and reviews.

For information, please address the author at 408 Phoenix Avenue, NW, Albuquerque, New Mexico, 87107.

FIRST EDITION

This book has been reviewed by a Roman Catholic Censure for theological accuracy. All scripture quoted is from The New American Bible: Copyright 2002 United States Conference of Catholic Bishops. Used by permission

Library of Congress Cataloging-in-Publication Data
Ponce, Jose Antonio.
   Modern Catholic Prayers by Jose Antonio Ponce
   ISBN 971-1-7351855-1-4
     1. Religion
     2. Spirituality
     3. Prayers
Printed in the United States of America

10 9 8 7 6 5 4 3 2 1

Jose Antonio Ponce

For my mother Margaret and my father Jesus, who made sure that I was raised Catholic and never abandoned me or their faith despite the difficult times they often faced.

Table of Contents

Introduction

1.-Lord, Help Me to Pray

5.-Sacramental Prayers

21.-Prayers of Praise

39.-Prayers of Thanksgiving

57.-Prayers of Confession

101.-Prayers of Supplication

153.-Prayers of Intercession and Petition

184.-Afterword

Dear reader,

For a Christian, prayer is simply talking with God. That master of prayer, St. Teresa of Avila, summed it up so beautifully: "Prayer is nothing else but being on terms of friendship with God, frequently conversing in secret with Him."

It is this spirit of prayer that I found in this collection of prayer by my friend and parishioner, Jose Antonio Ponce. They are the unaffected words of one heart speaking to another Heart of the joys, sorrows, and questions of life. That is what makes them so moving.

The content of the prayers are fully in accord with the Catholic faith that we both share and love, but there is nothing "narrow" about them. They will speak to the heart of every believer.

All of the prayers are of great value, but I was particularly moved by the prayer for after a suicide. To have a loved one take his or her life is shattering for those left behind. To find the words to speak to God about this can be very hard. I found Jose Antonio's prayers for this delicate subject very moving and healing.

When you pray these prayers, make sure to leave time to listen in the quiet of your heart for the voice of God. Our biggest challenge in prayer is not finding the right words to say to God, but allowing the time of silence to listen to the words God says to us.

May God bless all those who read and pray from this book.

(The Rev. Msgr.) Douglas A. Raun
October 24, 2021

Pray without ceasing.-1 Thessalonians. 5:17

Lord, help me to pray

Lord, help me to pray
for peace,
for comfort,
for love,
for solace.

help me to pray for courage,
for strength,
for patience
and for hope.

give me prayers of praise,
of adoration,
admiration and glory

lead me to pray for grace,
for consolation,
for redemption,
forgiveness and compassion

may my prayers bring
humility,
clarity,
wonder
and assurance.

you are the creator,

Modern Catholic Prayers

Jose Antonio Ponce

the master of thought,
of language,
of expression

please, Lord,
give me the wisdom to pray fruitfully
so that all of creation may be lifted
and give glory to your name.

amen

Modern Catholic Prayers

Jose Antonio Ponce

Be eager to present yourself as acceptable to God, a workman who causes no disgrace, imparting the word of truth without deviation.- 2 Timothy 2:15

Sacramental Prayers

Sacraments of Initiation

Baptismal Prayer
Confirmation Prayer
Eucharistic Prayer

Sacraments of Healing

Prayer of Penance
Anointing of the Sick

Sacraments of Service

Marriage Prayer
Holy Orders Prayer

This prefigured baptism, which saves you now. It is not a removal of dirt from the body but an appeal to God for a clear conscience, through the resurrection of Jesus Christ, who has gone into heaven and is at the right hand of God.- 1 Peter 3:21-22

Baptismal Prayer

it is the first sign of faith
that we are baptized to the Lord
dedicated to Jesus Christ
made ready for the Holy Spirit

this choice to do his will
preferring to remain inviolate
choosing life over death
sets us apart from the world

this promise made willingly
or put forth by our parents
gives us the salvation
guaranteed to all
who would do God's will

it is a way back when we fall
a way forward in difficult times
a means to be made whole
a path to eternal life

may we live out our baptismal promises

to renounce evil
to believe in God
remember him
keep his commandments
and always serve him

through the baptism of water and the Holy Spirit
in communion with God the Father
his son, Jesus Christ
and the Holy Spirit
we are made whole

amen

Do not let this book of the law depart from your lips. Recite it by day and by night, that you may carefully observe all that is written in it; then you will attain your goal; then you will succeed. I command you: be strong and steadfast! Do not fear nor be dismayed, for the LORD, your God, is with you wherever you go.-
Joshua 1:9

Confirmation Prayer

we are prepared now
for spiritual warfare
marked now
with the blood of Christ

we make this commitment
to serve God
to defend his word

we have grown as Christians
and are now
sent out into the world
as soldiers of Christ
accepting our responsibility
to the gospel, the faith and the ministry

bestow on us, Lord
the gifts of the Holy Spirit
charity,
joy, peace,

patience,
benignity, goodness,
long-suffering,
mildness, faith,
modesty, continency
and chastity

give us the strength
to resist temptation
to defend the innocent
redeem the fallen
and seek justice for the injured

may we always defend you
through suffering and sorrow

amen

Jesus said to them, "Amen, amen, I say to you, it was not Moses who gave the bread from heaven; my Father gives you the true bread from heaven. For the bread of God is that which comes down from heaven and gives life to the world.- John 6:33

Eucharistic Prayer

you, Lord
are the living bread
the salvation of the world

I have confessed my sins,
prepared my heart
and am ready to accept you
so that you might
fulfill the promise you made
on Calvary

you did not abandon us
after your resurrection
but left this sacrament
so that we might know you more intimately

you became human, oh Lord
so that we might share in your divinity
that we might become incorruptible
once again

help me to receive you with confidence
that I may know you completely

Modern Catholic Prayers

Jose Antonio Ponce

in the breaking of the bread
may I always remember
your sacrifice
that you have shared yourself
and have offered us eternity

amen

If we acknowledge our sins, he is faithful and just and will forgive our sins and cleanse us from every wrongdoing. - 1 John 1:9

Prayer of Penance

each day I struggle, Lord
to keep your commandments
and each day I fail

but your grace is sufficient
and your mercy boundless
so that each blemish
is removed from my soul
and cast into the nothingness
never to be remembered

do not let sin remind me of my failings
instead, let my sin remind me of your sacrifice
I know that I am forgiven
that I am released
that death will not touch me

I want to be whole again
alive in your spirit
unburdened of my sin

I resolve to be mindful
of my weakness
to think before I act

wanting never to fall into darkness again

let me be perfected,
purified
so that your compassion
your glory,
your truth
are a light for the world
through me

amen

Is anyone among you suffering? He should pray. Is anyone in good spirits? He should sing praise. Is anyone among you sick? He should summon the presbyters of the church, and they should pray over him and anoint him with oil in the name of the Lord, and the prayer of faith will save the sick person, and the Lord will raise him up. If he has committed any sins, he will be forgiven. James 5:13-15

Anointing of the Sick

Lord,
you eased the suffering of many
in your lifetime

you healed each one individually
with a touch,
a word,
a breath,
a thought

those who suffer
have faith
in your healing touch
and in you
the promise of resurrection
a world without pain

by their anointing
we strengthen them
and bring them into your presence

remind them of your own suffering
and give them the hope of new life
let my hands be your hands
guiding them to you
and reminding them
that the pain of this world
is fleeting

amen

Enjoy life with the wife you love, all the days of the vain life granted you under the sun.- Ecclesiastes 9:9

Your every act should be done with love.- 1 Corinthians 16:14

Marriage Prayer

we have found one another
and blessed our love through your union
together we will be stronger
an unbroken cord

with you as our foundation, Lord
we will stand firm against temptation
seeking only your grace

your promise to bless us
for our faithfulness
now increased twofold
that our lives may increase

show us the way to teach our children
to lead others through love
to your grace

to truly live out your word
that two shall be as one

amen

When Samuel went to sleep in his place, the Lord came and stood there, calling out as before: Samuel, Samuel! Samuel answered, "Speak, for your servant is listening." 1 Samuel:9-10

Then I heard the voice of the Lord saying, "Whom shall I send? Who will go for us?" "Here I am," I said; "send me!"-Isaiah 6:8

Holy Orders

I have answered your call, Lord

for some reason
you have set me apart
asked me to know you further
so that I may lead your people

an unworthy servant
I am ready to be shaped
an empty vessel
waiting to be filled with your wisdom
a catalyst for your grace

always remind me
to be humble
to be just
to be compassionate
to be courageous

and to be loving

this is my most sacred vow, Lord
that I will defend your word

may your love be reflected in me
so that others may come to know you
through your word
your life
and your sacrifice

amen

Praise is the form of prayer which recognizes most immediately that God is God. It lauds God for his own sake and gives him glory, quite beyond what he does, but simply because HE IS. It shares in the blessed happiness of the pure of heart who love God in faith before seeing him in glory. - Catechism of the Catholic Church-Part IV Christian Prayer Paragraph 2639

Prayers of Praise and Adoration

Prayer in Praise of God's Creation
God's Presence
The Majesty of God's Voice
Prayer in Praise of Freedom
Prayer in Praise of God's Word
Prayer in Praise of the Holy Trinity
Prayer in Praise of the Sabbath
Prayer in Praise of Faith

When I see your heavens, the work of your fingers, the moon and stars that you set in place. What is man that you are mindful of him, and a son of man that you care for him? Yet you have made him little less than a god, crowned him with glory and honor. You have given him rule over the works of your hands, put all things at his feet: All sheep and oxen, even the beasts of the field, The birds of the air, the fish of the sea, and whatever swims the paths of the seas! Psalm 8:4-9

Prayer in Praise of God's Creation

how wondrous is the universe
set in motion with your thought
perfectly brought forth
everything in existence
designed to fit your plan

surrounded by a blanket of magnificent stars
in an unfathomable vastness,
incredible beauty and desolation
the sun warms
the moon sets the tides
the waters perfectly balanced to provide rain

the light and the darkness,
the seasons,
precisely conceived
to bring forth and sustain life in every form

every creature, every soul
each with purpose

part of the grandeur,
the splendor
of your handiwork

you have painted the world
with unimaginable beauty
a palette of colors, textures
sights, sounds,
flavors and aromas
all for our delight

you have given us this wealth to enjoy
to care for and to manage
trusted us with your creation
knowing that we will someday live up to the task
of becoming the custodians of your imagination

finally, you have bestowed upon us
imagination and resourcefulness
with which we ourselves can create

Lord God,
surrounded by this beauty
we are too often unaware of your presence in all things
overwhelmed by the subtle elegance or this world

let me never deny your creation
always giving you honor and glory
for this gift bestowed

amen

Jose Antonio Ponce

Ever since the creation of the world, his invisible attributes of eternal power and divinity have been able to be understood and perceived in what he has made. as a result, they have no excuse.- Romans 1:20

God's Presence

you are present in everything, oh Lord
there is nothing on this earth
or in the heavens
that is not of your handiwork

in nature,
your perfect glory is revealed daily
the earth is clothed with the sun,
adorned with beauty
and cast into the heavens, a jewel unsurpassed

man's creation cannot compare to yours
your presence remains within us
even those things that man has corrupted
reveal your bearing

what we have plundered
you have restored
those whom we have abandoned
you have rescued

your spirit remains always
a lifeline of hope

it cannot be destroyed
will not be ignored
and shall never be withdrawn

you, our god, do not abandon us
even when we turn away

grant us the wisdom to recognize you
in all that surrounds us
to find that part of you that persists
and draws us ever closer to you

amen

Listen to his angry voice and the rumble that comes forth from his mouth! Everywhere under the heavens he sends it, with his light, to the ends of the earth. Again, his voice roars, his majestic voice thunders; he does not restrain them when his voice is heard. God thunders forth marvels with his voice;.- Job 37:2-5

The Majesty of God's Voice

I hear your thunder
roaring from the heavens
frightening and majestic
a reminder of your power

a flash of lightening
the brilliance of your thought
a prelude to the gift of
powerful song

I see the gathering storm
obedient
never doubting, never questioning

each drop of rain
perfectly placed
the world renewed
by your cleansing grace

may I always hear
and obey your voice

Jose Antonio Ponce

in awe of your glory
earning your redemption
when I fall away
call to me, oh Lord
correct my steps
with your song

light my way
with your brilliance
hold me accountable
with the voice of correction

amen

The human heart plans the way, but the LORD directs the steps.-Proverbs 16:9

Prayer in Praise of Freedom

you, my Lord
who created the universe
filled it with wonder,
made man from the dust of the earth
and filled him with joy
you have offered us freedom

not in slavery
have you placed man
but rather, given him
the will to choose
only a loving father would do so

your love
patient,
kind and forgiving
a love of heartbreak
is freely given

yet, from our moment of awareness
we disappoint you
disobeying always for self
often for spite

still, you are there always
with open arms
never scolding

your salvation everlasting
allowing us to move forward
and make our choices
good or bad
again and again and again

thank you, Lord
for the freedom to choose
the freedom to be human
no matter how flawed
for, ultimately
we are your creation

amen

Jose Antonio Ponce

Indeed, the word of God is living and effective, sharper than any two-edged sword, penetrating even between soul and spirit, joints and marrow, and able to discern reflections and thoughts of the heart.- Hebrews 4:12

Prayer in Praise of God's Word

your word, Lord, is forever
the beginning and end
without your word
there is no creation

the heavens and all that surround us
owe their existence
to your very breath

your word spoke everything into being

in all of history
there has been no guiding wisdom
more precious than your word

the principles that guide man
the laws that govern
all spring from your mouth
first set in stone
and then revealed to all

without your word
we could not be free

Jose Antonio Ponce

to reject your word
is to enter into peril
for without this wisdom
we are lost
removed from your presence
and abandoned to our cruel desires

Lord, let us not refuse the love
revealed in your word

remain with us always

amen

In the foreknowledge of God the Father, through sanctification by the Spirit, for obedience and sprinkling with the blood of Jesus Christ: may grace and peace be yours in abundance.- 1 Peter 1:2

Prayer in Praise of the Holy Trinity

the greatest, most wonderful mystery
is the salvation of the world
the foundation for the faith that I adore

you have known us, father
before we came into being
creating the failsafe
for a flawed and weak race

at creation's dawning
you walked with us
as we explored your wonders
when we failed
you corrected and guided us with your mighty hand
your love and compassion
is our salvation

you gave your only begotten Son
as sacrifice for our sins
in the most horrible and painful way
so that we might not suffer eternally

when you called your son home
you left the Holy Spirit
as protector,

as conscience
and guide
a mighty advocate
providing enduring courage and wisdom
until we once again
stand in your presence
made whole by your love

oh, blessed trinity
save us from our sins

amen

Jose Antonio Ponce

If you refrain from trampling the sabbath, from following your own pursuits on my holy day; If you call the sabbath a delight, the Lord's holy day glorious; If you glorify it by not following your ways, seeking your own interests, or pursuing your own affairs. Then you shall delight in the Lord, and I will make you ride upon the heights of the earth; I will nourish you with the heritage of Jacob, your father, for the mouth of the Lord has spoken.-Isaiah 58:13-14

Prayer in Praise of the Sabbath

you rested, God
pursued nothing further
on the seventh day
taking in all of creation

this day is set aside for praise
for wonder and reflection

we have lost our innocence
treating your day as any other
buying and selling
ignoring your handiwork

help me, Lord, to see your creation
to understand your word
to heed your call

on this day
give me strength
of renewed spirit
let me be your servant

Modern Catholic Prayers

Jose Antonio Ponce

so that your courage
your strength
your magnificence
may shine through me every day

may the glory of who you are
give my tongue cause to sing
of your creation

amen

For, if you confess with your mouth that Jesus is Lord and believe in your heart that God raised him from the dead, you will be saved.-Romans 10:9

Prayer in Praise of Faith

you, Lord, have bestowed a knowledge and faith
available to all

your redemption so horribly offered
so viciously fulfilled
purchased for us our souls

from that sacrifice
comes joy, peace
and a comfort

your resurrection
confirms my faith
I have been rescued and renewed
touched by the light of your grace

I seek only to believe
and to pass this faith on to others

amen

Modern Catholic Prayers

Jose Antonio Ponce

A psalm of thanksgiving. Shout joyfully to the Lord, all you lands; serve the Lord with gladness; come before him with joyful song. Know that the Lord is God, he made us, we belong to him, we are his people, the flock he shepherds. Enter his gates with thanksgiving, his courts with praise. Give thanks to him, bless his name; good indeed is the Lord, His mercy endures forever, his faithfulness lasts through every generation.- Psalm 100:1-5

Prayers of Thanks

Prayer of Thanksgiving
Prayer in Thanks for Parents
Prayer of Thanks for Prayers Answered
Prayer of Thanks for Conviction
Prayer in Thanks for Forgiveness
Prayer of Thanks for a Godly Wife
Prayer of Thanks for Friends
Prayer of Thanks for Animal Companions

Have no anxiety at all, but in everything, by prayer and petition, with thanksgiving, make your requests known to God.- Philippians 4:6

Prayer of Thanksgiving

thank you, Lord for all I have

you have blessed me with friends and family
although I am flawed
they are with me for support
through love and conflict

thank you for my trials
for without difficulties
I might never triumph
nor understand the need for repentance and
forgiveness

thank you for the interactions I have daily
the casual acquaintances
the clerks and countermen
the more than patient bill collectors
the postmen,
bankers,
tax collectors
volunteers,
potential clients,
complaining customers,
unruly children
and enduring parents

thank you for music
glorious jazz,
soul
and rock and roll

for those who make-believe,
actors and authors
who spin a story
and create new worlds just for me

thank you for those little creatures
who are our friends
they teach us of your unconditional love
with a kiss, a nuzzle
or a well-placed paw

your world of delights
countless opportunities
un-told wealth of sights,
sounds, touch,
tastes and smells
remind me that you are the source of all things
great and small

amen

Children's children are the crown of the elderly, and the glory of children is their parentage. Proverbs 17:6

Prayer in Thanksgiving for Parents

Lord,
without my parents,
I may not have found you

their instruction,
example and patience
allows me now to stand in your presence
asking for your grace and forgiveness

there were moments
when I tried my parents' patience,
deeply disappointed,
angered and confused them with my behavior

still, I was always able to look to them
for compassion,
love and hope
and was never turned away
even as an adult

your design of family is flawless
your instruction perfect
for those who would listen
and heed your word

in a perfect world
families take care of

and protect one another
in this world set on destruction
family and faith are all that can save us

help me to be a parent to my children
and to all in need of family
whether stranger or friend

amen

But he should ask in faith, not doubting, for the one who doubts is like a wave of the sea that is driven and tossed about by the wind. For that person must not suppose that he will receive anything from the Lord, since he is a man of two minds, unstable in all his ways.-James 1:6-8

Prayer of Thanks for Prayers Answered

you have heard and answered me
giving me strength to continue

my life,
corrupt and spoiled
you love and find worthy
your compassion overwhelms me
I weep with joy

despite my cruel nature
you have redeemed me
and continue to love and forgive me

so often I call upon you
yet fail to listen
denied your counsel
expecting salvation
from the turmoil I have created

not asking with faith
that might give you glory
but rather as a spoiled child

Jose Antonio Ponce

expecting a father's indulgence

still,
you have found it in your heart
to ease my burden
and create a refuge
from the sins I have committed
against myself,
my brother and you

please do not stop listening
and keep me in your heart
until I am your perfect servant

amen

Therefore all you have brought upon us, all you have done to us, you have done by a proper judgment.- Daniel 3:31

Prayer of Thanks for Conviction

I have sinned, Lord
a sin that has led me to ruin
and yet you have taken pity on me

the free will bestowed
I have abused
the counsel offered
I have ignored
your intervention
through friends and relatives
I have rejected

I find myself the victim of my actions
your justice meted out
through my own foolishness

my conviction
is a blessing
an opportunity to begin again
a choice forced upon me
by my stubbornness

there are clear decisions here
between love and loss
faith and folly
life and death

Lord,
guide me once again
remind me of your faithfulness
envelop me in your mercy

let your justice resolve my sin
may the consequences of my actions
reveal my sin
so that I may amend my behavior
and glorify you through change

amen

Jose Antonio Ponce

Christ Jesus came into the world to save sinners. Of these I am the foremost. But for that reason I was mercifully treated, so that in me, as the foremost, Christ Jesus might display all his patience as an example for those who would come to believe in him for everlasting life.-1 Timothy:15-16

Prayer in Thanks for Forgiveness

I am grateful, Lord, for your mercy
and forgiveness.

without your grace, I am lost forever
my failings recalled daily
my weakness,
my sins,
my willfulness exposed

I am reminded
of the sin that possesses me
of the things I have done
and conspire to do

none are worthy of your compassion
I, least deserving of all

you have reached out to me
in the depths of my affliction
brought me healing and comfort
and have made me whole
again and again

you bestow your gracious love upon me

obliterating my sin
you sacrificed your son on the cross
defeating my enemy for me

may your forgiveness compel me
to remain faithful,
to avoid sin
so that I may not suffer under your justice

do not condemn me, Lord
allow me to live within your mercy
forever and ever

amen

Happy the man who lives with a sensible woman.
Sirach 25:8

A wife is her husband's richest treasure, a help like himself and a staunch support. Sirach 36:29

Prayer of Thanks for a Godly Wife

my wife is my treasure
presented to me by the living God
who wants only the best for me

she tempers my recklessness
keeps my foolish thoughts at bay
and stands with me through all of my trials

without her
who knows where I would be?

not every man needs a wife
nor every woman a husband
but those who are joined in marriage
are wise to choose a Godly spouse

having made poor choices in the past
this prize is much more valuable to me
my wife did not abandon me in my sin,
in my times of weakness

instead, she forgave me
choosing patience over rejection

Jose Antonio Ponce

correcting and offering
the chance to grow and believe with her
that I could be a better man,
husband and father

I have accepted love
and shall never be alone
until she returns home to her God
to prepare a place for me
in God's heaven

amen

Happy the one who finds a friend, who speaks to attentive ears. Sirach 25:9

Prayer of Thanks for Friends

I am surrounded, Lord, by your grace

you have given me
friends who love and support me

they listen
often without judgement
always with care and concern
and correct me when I stray from your word

we laugh and cry
and grow old together
we learn from one another

many are the gifts they bring
honesty,
sympathy,
joy

some are lifetime friends
others I have had for too brief a time
each cherished
as a gift of your love

they are a refuge for me

Modern Catholic Prayers

Jose Antonio Ponce

a place where I am always welcome
respite from an often-difficult journey
keeping loneliness at bay

they give my life meaning
and make me feel that I matter

bless these messengers of your good will
for all of their good works

amen

Jose Antonio Ponce

But now ask the beasts to teach you, the birds of the air to tell you; Or speak to the earth to instruct you, and the fish of the sea to inform you. Which of all these does not know that the hand of God has done this?-Job 12:7-9

Prayer of Thanks for Animal Companions

Lord,
you provide animals
to nourish us
help us carry our load
make our lives easier

but an equally great gift
is their wisdom
they teach us of your unconditional love
bring us joy
are beside us in sorrow
and do not abandon us in crisis

you have chosen the smallest of creatures
to set an example
of how we should treat one another
how we should love
without reservation or regret
it is the pure love
of salvation

amen

Modern Catholic Prayers

Jose Antonio Ponce

Therefore, confess your sins to one another and pray for one another, that you may be healed. The fervent prayer of a righteous person is very powerful. - James 5:16

Prayers of Confession

Lament of the Fig Tree
Prayer for Intercession Against the World
Prayer to Guard Against Greed
Prayer to Overcome
Prayer of the Fallen Man
Prayer to Return to God
Prayer of the Ungrateful Man
Prayer for Resistance to Sexual Addiction
Prayer of the Divorced
Prayer of Addiction
Prayer for Deliverance from Greed
Prayer for Financial Responsibility
Prayer for Rescue from Darkness
Prayer to Resist Jealousy
The Liars Prayer
Prayer for the Strength to Forgive
Prayer of the Unfulfilled
Prayer of Failure
Prayer for Renewed Faith
The Doubters Prayer

And he told them this parable: "There once was a person who had a fig tree planted in his orchard, and when he came in search of fruit on it but found none, he said to the gardener, 'For three years now I have come in search of fruit on this fig tree but have found none. So cut it down. Why should it exhaust the soil?' He said to him in reply, 'Sir, leave it for this year also, and I shall cultivate the ground around it and fertilize it; it may bear fruit in the future. If not, you can cut it down.'"- Luke 13:6-9

Lament of the Fig Tree

I am the fig tree
bearing no fruit
season after season

and you, the vinedresser
continue to nourish me
hoping for a change

lead me toward a greater faith
into holiness
and away from sin

with your blade
cut away those things in my life
that keep me from serving you completely
so that I may give glory to your name

amen

Jose Antonio Ponce

For many, as I have often told you and now tell you even in tears, conduct themselves as enemies of the cross of Christ. Their end is destruction. Their God is their stomach; their glory is in their "shame." Their minds are occupied with earthly things.-Philippians 3:17-19

Prayer for Intercession Against the World

oh God, humble me.
preserve me from my own destruction

let me turn away from my own comfort
and from my sin
for your sake and the sake of others.

the world blinds me to your grace and mercy
I have turned my face away from you
have ignored your pleas to return to you

this world's temptations
have removed you from my field of vision
blinding me to truth,
to love,
to forgiveness

let me not boast of my misdeeds,
my indulgence,
my sin,
as a drunkard boasts of his consumption

but rather,
help me to fill my life

with promises made and fulfilled
to your glory.

fill my mind,
my heart, my soul
with your presence
and a love for you
that challenges and conquers
all earthly intent.

amen

Then he said to the crowd, "Take care to guard against all greed, for though one may be rich, one's life does not consist of possessions." -Luke 12:15

Prayer to Guard Against Greed

I want more and more and more
of things that in the end,
have no real value

all I own
will become worthless
none of these shall save me
from illness,
from sorrow,
from loneliness,
from grief

possessions provide temporary distraction
from the true treasure that surrounds me

I have lost my way
am blind to your creation
what you have created, Lord
no man can imitate

I am tethered to hardware

help me to realize that
all is fleeting
possessions worthless

Jose Antonio Ponce

let me seek only your grace

give me courage
to proclaim your word
so that the true treasure
may be known to all

amen

Because he himself was tested through what he suffered, he is able to help those who are being tested..- Hebrews 2:18

Prayer to Overcome

Lord,
take away my temptations
relieve me of passions
that pull me down
into depravity
into selfish desires

remove these thorns

it is within your power
to make this so
for nothing is impossible with you

my desires are mis-directed
my focus,
my prayer
should be for courage,
for endurance
to resist sin
and keep from falling into the world

to give glory to you
by overcoming evil
no matter how small
will prove to the world
that you are the answer to all prayers

Jose Antonio Ponce

Lord,
help me to find that courage
and through my actions
inspire others to do the same

amen

Rescue me from the mire, and do not let me sink.
Rescue me from those who hate me and from the
watery depths -Psalms 69:15

Prayer of the Fallen Man

Lord,
I continue to sin

I pray that this wickedness would leave me
but within the hour
I return to my offence

I am a poor husband and father,
a wretched son and brother,
an unfaithful servant
a thief, a liar and a selfish man

I fall, constantly
I continue to be caught up
in my heart and soul
with self
my mind turns hourly to lust
I disgrace women
with thoughts that exploit them

I find comfort in things
and covet what I do not have
I seek possessions
rather than your grace

I am envious of those
who have earned their leisure
and curse them for their diligence

I curse myself
for not demanding more of myself
in my youth

I have squandered
the life and the talents
bestowed upon me

those gifts,
wither and die
like a neglected garden
I have nothing
with which to repay you

my mind is in constant worry

I serve money
I want only for myself
and discard everyone else

I have so ruined myself
that I don't fit anywhere
nor with anyone

I make more of myself than I am
with lies and boasting

I pray that my sins may see the light of day

Modern Catholic Prayers

Jose Antonio Ponce

and that I may be cleansed
by the truth

you give all to me
and I have repaid you
with selfishness
with scorn

I understand your word
I know that I can be forgiven
seventy times seven

I am fallen, Lord
save me

amen

Jose Antonio Ponce

Yet even now, oracle of the Lord, return to me with your whole heart, with fasting, weeping, and mourning. Rend your hearts, not your garments, and return to the Lord, your God, for he is gracious and merciful, slow to anger, abounding in steadfast love, and relenting in punishment. Perhaps he will again relent and leave behind a blessing, Grain offering and libation for the Lord, your God.- Joel 2:12-14

Prayer to Return to God

help me, Lord,
to return to you
with all my heart and soul
using every resource at my command
to give glory to your name.

the world's siren melody
rings constantly in my ears
compelling me not to desires of the spirit
but to the sins of the body
pulling me further and further away
from heaven

help me to remember
lessons learned as a child
about truth,
compassion,
mercy and love

give me the strength to fast and pray
with purpose and true love for you
instill in me the need for you

Jose Antonio Ponce

my world crumbles despite your clemency
you right my ship again and again
making me whole
despite my desire
for self-destruction.

aid me once again
in pulling myself from this cesspool of sin
and depravity
to try yet again
to earn the mercy you have always bestowed on me.

amen.

For by grace, you have been saved through faith, and this is not from you; it is the gift of God; it is not from works, so no one may boast Ephesians 2:8-9

Prayer of the Ungrateful Man

Lord,
you have rescued me from my foolishness,
counseled me in sorrow
and healed my wounds
only to be forgotten
in the next moment

I return to selfishness
making decisions that do not include you
attending to myself before others,
never giving thanks,
or praise,
or glory

I believe myself best suited
to the task of running my life
yet without exception,
I turn to you in my time of need
seeking justice, relief,
reward,
refreshment

once my need has been filled
my strength renewed
my crisis abated

Jose Antonio Ponce

I revert to sin
filled with vanity,
boasting of my accomplishments
and denying you like the poor apostle I am.

only my faith in your mercy
keeps me from destroying myself
may that faith in you
be enough to help me change

for I am lost without your grace.

amen

This is the will of God, your holiness: that you refrain from immorality, that each of you know how to acquire a wife for himself in holiness and honor, not in lustful passion as do the Gentiles who do not know God.- 1Thesselonians.4:3-5

Prayer for Resistance to Sexual Addiction

my life has been lived in lust
from that first temptation
and lapse of temperance
through my latest sin

I equate the sexual experience
with the spiritual experience
and use that reasoning
for my own sordid purposes.

I don't always act
on my near constant carnal thoughts
I know that I am
a touch,
a kiss,
a conversation away
from debasing myself
and another, perhaps, more innocent person.

Jesus, remove from me this weakness
this addiction to the flesh
show me the way out of my sin
and give me the grace to resist temptation.

Modern Catholic Prayers

Jose Antonio Ponce

help me to respect my body
and the physical personhood of others
remind me that they too, are your temple
your dwelling place
and that their spirit belongs to you
so that I may not lead others into sin

in your name oh heavenly father,

amen

He said to them, "Because of the hardness of your hearts Moses allowed you to divorce your wives, but from the beginning it was not so.- Matthew 19:8

Prayer of the Divorced

I have turned away from my vows
leaving behind my spouse
my family

how can I be forgiven?

because of desire
or my own selfish nature
I left my home
and now I feel regret

many suffered because of my decision
children,
siblings,
parents, friends

I lacked the patience and courage
to work on the problems in my marriage
and simply walked away

with a more mature soul
I know where I went wrong
I failed to trust in you, Lord
in your institution of marriage
created for us perfectly
as you are perfect

Jose Antonio Ponce

I cannot undo the damage
nor heal the hurt
I created for my family
but from this day forward
with your guidance
help me to move toward reconciliation
and care of my family
and remain faithful to your precepts
in any new relationships

amen

No trial has come to you but what is human. God is faithful and will not let you be tried beyond your strength; but with the trial he will also provide a way out, so that you may be able to bear it. 1 Corinthians.10:13

Prayer of Addiction

Lord, I am sick
I wake up sick
and I go to bed sick

I crave poison
my whole body wants,
seeks,
its own destruction

I have fallen into a world of iniquity
a weight pulls at me
with each step I take

I can't concentrate
I can't remember
I can't function

my only thought
is how
and where
and when
relief will come

I have ruined everything

Jose Antonio Ponce

I steal all that I can
and return nothing
I shame myself and those around me

without your healing hand
to comfort me
to give me the strength and resolve
to overcome,
to resist,
to ask for help

I will sink further and further
into darkness

Lord, save me from myself
give me the strength,
the resolve
to trust in you and your healing love
and to ask others for the help I need

amen

Modern Catholic Prayers

Jose Antonio Ponce

Those who want to be rich are falling into temptation and into a trap and into many foolish and harmful desires, which plunge them into ruin and destruction.
1 Timothy 6:9

Prayer for Deliverance from Greed

Lord,
greed temps me
and I see only too late
that it is the cause for every evil in the world.

none are immune to its allure
not priests,
presidents,
kings or servants.
all may become slaves to the demon
that is greed

it has caused me to betray those around me
abandon those that need me
steal from those who employ me
and deceive those who would assist me

my life has been lived for money
it brings untrue love
unworthy praise,
specious accomplishment

it carries with it pride and arrogance
and is the wheel of sin

Jose Antonio Ponce

driven to destruction
I have seen those in hunger suffer
while I gorge myself

those in need go without
while I waste all that is given to me
many have been crushed under the feet of my
opulence.

Lord,
let me redeem myself through faith,
charity, poverty and good works.
deliver me from destructive need,
and selfish gain.

let me go forth from this day
removing material indulgence,
placing value on giving,
delighting in want

forgive me for the sin of greed
and create in me a new heart
intent on giving

make me humble
serving those in need
and those who need me.

amen

Jose Antonio Ponce

The rich rule over the poor, and the borrower is the slave of the lender. Proverbs 22:7

Prayer for Financial Responsibility

I spend and I spend and I spend
money that should go to my responsibilities,
to the poor
and to your works, oh Lord

I seek comfort in possessions
I seek glory and praise from those
who believe that I am wealthier than I am

I spend without the thought of consequence
without regard for how my foolishness
affects others around me

so much could be accomplished
with only a small amount of restraint
but I seek to be noticed for what I can possess
rather than for who I am

worst of all
possessions lose their meaning
their value
once they are mine
they mock me
reminding me of my folly

Lord,
let judgement fall where it will

Jose Antonio Ponce

so that I might learn restraint
help me to make choices that are responsible
and righteous

lead me to offer you the first fruits of my wealth
and more
teach me to use my earnings
to care for those in need,
to invest in the good works of your apostles
so that your word
and your sacrifice
may be known to all

for it is only by your grace
that I have means at all

it is through charity
that we learn mercy
though want that we find true treasure
among those things that have meaning
and by letting go
that we begin to understand
the true nature of your benevolence

amen

Answer me, Lord, in your generous love; in your great mercy turn to me. Do not hide your face from your servant; hasten to answer me, for I am in distress. Come and redeem my life; because of my enemies ransom me. You know my reproach, my shame, my disgrace; before you stand all my foes. Insult has broken my heart, and I despair; I looked for compassion, but there was none, for comforters, but found none. -Psalm 69:17-21

Prayer for Rescue from the Darkness

Lord,
I have fallen into the world
a deep, dark cistern
that obscures your light

I hide my face from you in the darkness
and stumble about
searching for salvation
seeking comfort in temptation

in this world,
this blackness
lies are currency
selfishness and greed
are virtue

the world is deaf to my plea
becoming louder,
more distracting
removing even your faintest presence

I know that you are here
in the midst of darkness
and that if I stretch my arm toward you
with firm grasp
you will take hold
and rescue me from the filth that surrounds me

pick me up
forgive my sin
release me from guilt
and accept me, once again
as your child

for your compassion is boundless
your faith in your creation unceasing

formed in your image
we are nearer to perfection than we realize

closer to you than the rest of creation
if we would only be still
listen
and believe

amen

Jose Antonio Ponce

Anger is cruel, and wrath overwhelming, but before jealousy who can stand?- Proverbs 27:4

Prayer to Resist Jealousy

Lord,
my heart is full of jealousy
for those who have more than I
who have succeeded where I have failed

it resents the good fortune and hard work
of my contemporaries

I have no right to begrudge anyone
I have arrived at this destination
on my own
journeyed here
on a trail of my choosing

please help me to let go of my anger,
my jealousy,
my envy

help me to put to use the energy wasted in complaint
and anxiety about my situation
to further my goals

give me the proper patience
to respect those around me
who have earned the right to a modestly good life

do not let me fall into the trap

of believing that possessions
are the treasure I should seek

grant me humility,
graciousness,
patience

help me to understand that by uplifting others
acknowledging and celebrating their accomplishments
that I am recognizing your works
through them
and celebrating your gifts
and your glory

amen

The false witness will not go unpunished, and whoever utters lies will not escape. Proverbs 19:5

The Liar's Prayer

I am wicked
twisted from the womb
unable to speak the truth

I steal the accomplishments of others
and make them my own
I lie to create the illusion
that I am more than I am

I have acted in a cowardly fashion
placing blame where it does not belong
to save myself from the exposition of my dishonesty

deceit carries me headlong into the sins
of theft and pride
adultery and drunkenness

by outward appearance I am
humble, modest,
honest, charitable
but I am quick to judge
envious, jealous, angry,
spreading lies about those more accomplished
to lower them
in the eyes of others

I see the destruction my lies have caused

Jose Antonio Ponce

the unjustified faith
that people have in me

my cowardice keeps me from
making straight the crooked tapestry I have weaved
I fear retribution, recrimination
fear that I cannot be forgiven
never repay
nor repair the damage I've done

I have ensnared so many
with my evil tongue

please, Lord
give me the courage
to apologize for the wrong I have done
for my own self-serving desires

forgive those I have incited to sin
those I have encouraged, deceived, enabled
so that I might not be alone in my misery

make me pitiable if need be
take me down to nothing
so that I may be punished for my pride

still my lying tongue
forgive me my deceit
and lead me to righteousness
by your grace

amen

It is good sense to be slow to anger, and an honor to overlook an offense. Proverbs 19:11

Prayer for the Strength to Forgive

my life has been upended
an obscene offense has been committed against me
no salve can heal this pain
nor quench my anger

how this could have happened?
it doesn't make sense
there is no reason for this crime
for the loss
none can explain it to my satisfaction

I want those responsible
to suffer as we have suffered
I want justice beyond equity
I want vengeance

only you, my God
can subdue this pain,
can quell this rage,
pull this hatred from me

your love and strength
will guide me to forgiveness
that will lead me
eventually,
to peace

we will never forget
the sin committed here
it must be remembered
so that it will not be repeated

thank you, Lord,
for your love and compassion
restraint,
justice,
and peace

amen

Jose Antonio Ponce

By day may the Lord send his mercy, and by night may his righteousness be with me! I will pray to the God of my life, I will say to God, my rock: "Why do you forget me? Why must I go about mourning with the enemy oppressing me?" It shatters my bones, when my adversaries reproach me, when they say to me every day: "Where is your God?" Why are you downcast, my soul, why do you groan within me? Wait for God, for I shall again praise him, my savior and my God.
Psalm 42:9-12

Prayer of the Unfulfilled

oh, Lord
my life seems a waste
years and years of standing still
while the rest of the world blazes past me

I see my peers
moving ever forward
while I struggle to find my way

I see wicked men succeed
and good men fail
I am depressed and afraid to move

I feel abandoned and misused
unable to discern
your purpose for me

I have set myself on a path
away from you
lost my direction, my reason to be

fill me with your Holy Spirit
guide me,
through prayer
a way back to my being
an understanding of my meaning

make me resilient
give me patience
help me to persevere
and follow your instruction
so that I may be where I belong
a part of your plan

amen

But he said to me, "My grace is sufficient for you, for power is made perfect in weakness." I will rather boast most gladly of my weaknesses, in order that the power of Christ may dwell with me. Therefore, I am content with weaknesses, insults, hardships, persecutions, and constraints, for the sake of Christ; for when I am weak, then I am strong..-2 Corinthians 12:9-10

Prayer of Failure

Lord, I will return to you and fail
I will embrace your law and fail
will give up my sin and fail

with each heartbeat
I am one step closer to death,
one second, one hour, one day
closer to your justice

yet you offer your forgiveness
over and over

all that I need do is reach out
and you are there

why do so many resolve their sin
and I do not?

why do so many heed your word
while I am not able to keep the smallest of your commandments?

why do I fail again and again
where others repent and are saved?

my lusts control me
my fears guide me
my sin condemns me

please do not withdraw from me
let me come to you again and again
asking for your forgiveness
until I am healed
and am proof of your glory

amen

Faith is the realization of what is hoped for and evidence of things not seen.-Hebrews 11:1

Prayer for Renewed Faith

somewhere along the way
I replaced my faith in you
with faith in the world

I put aside your wisdom
believing my own would suffice
that I could adequately fulfill your role
as master of all,that surrounds me

in a moment of hubris
I believed that I could find solutions
without your guidance

I put my trust
in science,
in mysticism,
in things learned from the world

as I saw others succeed without you
I believed that only human wisdom was necessary
but I was wrong

you are the source of all wisdom

please forgive my stubbornness
my arrogance in believing that I

could master your universe
when it is clear that I cannot
manage even my own thoughts

renew my faith
rekindle my passion
for your knowledge
bring me home

amen

But without faith it is impossible to please him, for anyone who approaches God must believe that he exists and that he rewards those who seek him.- Hebrews 11:6

Doubters Prayer

doubt rises inside me
I am harassed on every side
by a world that professes to know the truth

I know the flaws history contains
and the mistakes made when transcribing your word
but I also know that your word is inviolate
and has been proven throughout history

still….
science offers answers
to questions I have always had
logic deems it necessary for me
to have an open mind
but how open?
how receptive?

your word is challenged at every turn
new explanations for your creation
theories and suppositions
that seem to make sense

Lord,
help me to find the answers in your word

seeking daily to understand you
and your creation
give me the knowledge
to defend and minister
to all those around me

especially those like me
who have doubt

amen

Modern Catholic Prayers

Jose Antonio Ponce

Have no anxiety at all, but in everything, by prayer and petition, with thanksgiving, make your requests known to God. - Philippians 4:6

Prayers of Supplication

Prayer for Redemption
Prayer for Courage
Prayer for the Lost
Prayer for Salvation for the World
Prayer to Hear God's Call
Prayer to Seek God
Prayer to Truly Know God
Prayer to Put on the Armor of God
Prayer to be Ready
Prayer for a Joyful Heart
Prayer for a Modest Life
The Step-Parents' Prayer
Prayer to be a Good Worker
Prayer of the Unemployed
Prayer for Deliverance from Fear
A Soldier's Prayer
Prayer of Soldiers Suffering from Post-Traumatic Stress
Prayer for Redemption from Agoraphobia
Prayer to Make Wise Choices
Prayer for a Satisfied Mind
Prayer for Relief from Regret
Prayer for Relief from Physical Affliction
Prayer for Relief from Worry

All have sinned and are deprived of the glory of God.- Romans 3:23

Let that be the prayer of the LORD's redeemed, those redeemed from the hand of the foe,-Psalm 107:2

Prayer for Redemption

Lord, redeem us
save us from sin
help me walk upright in your word

our prayers go unheeded
our questions unanswered
your eyes do not see us
we are lost in darkness

we pay lip service
observing the rites of faith
in our hearts

we have abandoned you

your saints were tempted
yet ultimately redeemed
but comparisons
with those whom you have chosen to lead
to instruct
would be yet another sin

our lives are corrupt
outside of your will

those looking for guidance
examine your flawed servants
and see a distorted reflection of you, my God

let no one be turned away from you
by our poisonous sins
chastise us, oh Lord
make us whole again

give us the faith
to walk away from sin
and mirror your grace

amen

"I have told you this so that you might have peace in me. In the world you will have trouble, but take courage, I have conquered the world."-John 16:33

Prayer for Courage

everyday requires courage
to resist temptations big and small
to stand up to tyranny
racism, inequity

we see these things
yet let them go by
as if they belong in this world
never thinking to stand in the gap
and stand up for God

Lord, give us the courage
to speak up
to take action
to set right the world
to find something that we can contribute
that will further the cause of justice

your world,
perfectly created,
has become corrupt
not through action but inaction
each standing aside
remaining solitary
in a world that needs community

help us to restore your world,
to the greater glory for which it was created
putting aside our weakness
replacing it with the strength you offer
in the spirit of your commandment
to love our neighbor as ourself

for we are your glory
when we do your will
and preserve out brothers and sisters

amen

For by grace, you have been saved through faith, and this is not from you; it is the gift of God. -Ephesians 2:8

Prayer for Salvation for the World

Lord,
we have forsaken you
for wretched treasures
lost our way
installed ourselves as gods
and turned away from your face

lost in self, greed, lust and cruelty
none is set above us

can we create beauty?
improve on your handiwork?

long ago, you kept your promise
that we would not be abandoned
would not be left to the slaughter

you sent your son to the gallows
for the sins of all mankind
so that just a word,
just a single thought of you
would bring redemption

without the fulfillment of that promise
there would be no hope

no exit from this cesspool of self

we must return to you
find the way back to the cross
kneel at its foot
and ask for forgiveness

we must turn away from the world
place ourselves under your scrutiny
knowing that your justice
is mercy, is salvation

help us to carry that message of truth
to the rest of the world
proclaiming your love
your glory
your redemption

guide us into seeing ourselves as we are
and the world as it is
expose our cruelty
our greed, our hubris

bring us to truth
and an understanding of your love
help us to turn the tide of oppression
to create a world where you are the center
and your love is truly
the salvation of the world

amen

Modern Catholic Prayers

Jose Antonio Ponce

So, for one who knows the right thing to do and does not do it, it is a sin. James 4:17

Prayer for the Lost

heavenly father
we are lost

the world continues to spin out of control
our sin dragging us down
our pride removing our guilt

we have no shame,
no remorse
for the things we do

we justify our behavior
believing ourselves to be in control
making decisions that affect
not only our souls
but the souls of others

we are un-redeemable

our only hope
is that you will look beyond our sin
to your sacrifice

that your compassion
will look away from our sin
and reclaim us

Modern Catholic Prayers

Jose Antonio Ponce

we may never find our way back to you
on our own

we are too far fallen
too long removed from your grace

amen

Ever since the creation of the world, his invisible attributes of eternal power and divinity have been able to be understood and perceived in what he has made. As a result, they have no excuse.-Romans 1:20

Prayer to Hear God's Call

all have ignored your call
again and again and again

we have knelt in your house
listening to your word
and walked away
discarding your grace
to walk our paths of destruction

we have closed our hearts
turned our backs
like petulant children
running from our father's voice

we are without reason
pulled away by the world

Lord,
make us receptive
to your word

give us wisdom to hear
discernment to understand your purpose
to better heed your call

Jose Antonio Ponce

you have called each of your children
there is no greater or lesser in you
each task you set before us
attests to your glory

let us diminish
while you increase
and let your glory shine
through the works you have asked of us

amen

Seek the Lord while he may be found; call on him while he is near. Isaiah 55:6

Prayer to Seek God

you, Lord are reality
unseen yet experienced
intangible but concrete

seduced by the world are we
pulled in every direction
offered countless paths
leading away from you

finding you should be easy
but even amongst your followers
there are disagreements
indefensible evil in our midst

keep us mindful
that men do not always represent you
that we are weak and imperfect
unable to get out of our own way

they would destroy your name
shield themselves from justice behind it
and use it for personal gain
and leave only your faithful to defend you

help us to persevere
to always seek your voice
in the cacophonous rhetoric that surrounds us

Jose Antonio Ponce

to defend you by faith and action

never let us lose sight of you
keep us always searching,
learning and growing in you
so that we might shine your light upon the world

amen

But rather, let those who boast, boast of this, that in their prudence they know me, Know that I, the Lord, act with fidelity, justice, and integrity on earth. How I take delight in these—oracle of the Lord.-Jeremiah 9:23-24

Prayer to Truly Know God

Lord, we see you
in all of creation
from sunrise to sunrise
your handiwork speaks

surrounded by your blessings
we are reminded of your love

but we do not know you
we hear your word
but often it does not live within us

we speak your name
but never speak with you

nor do we give praise to you
in the presence of our friends

our stubborn hearts
refuse to let go of our selfish nature

you have given all a choice
to decide right from wrong

Jose Antonio Ponce

you have paid the price
saved our souls

when you speak
let us hear you
instruct us

give us the patience for study
and the wisdom of understanding
for only then
may we truly know you

amen

So, stand fast with your loins girded in truth, clothed with righteousness as a breastplate, and your feet shod in readiness for the gospel of peace. In all circumstances, hold faith as a shield, to quench all the flaming arrows of the evil one. And take the helmet of salvation and the sword of the Spirit, which is the word of God. Constant Prayer. With all prayer and supplication, pray at every opportunity in the Spirit. Ephesians 6:14-17

Prayer to Put on the Armor of God

besieged and surrounded on all sides
our vulnerabilities exposed
weakness driving us to surrender
the world beguiles
fosters idleness and want
and pulls us further and further away from you

fear is a constant companion
we worry about money, work
and our own mortality

our flesh betrays our souls
with wanton thoughts,
shameless pride, envy and greed
destructive behavior that leads us to sin

lied to, easily persuaded
our failures displayed before all
the devil assures that we are not worthy
of your love, forgiveness, grace

discouraged, we are resigned to our fate

yet, seed has been planted in each of us
a kernel of faith, of understanding
that your mercy is infinite

inspired by your word
we are strengthened, emboldened
we move forward
knowing that your disciples were never abandoned
and that we are no less loved

the story is written
despite all of his conspiracies and deceptions
the devil is powerless
he assaulted you unto death
and was defeated by your resurrection

Lord, shield us daily with your word
grant us peace
save us from distraction,
from iniquity
and remind us always
that you are by our side
our defender,
our hope,
and our salvation

amen

For everyone who calls on the name of the Lord will be saved.-Romans 10:13

Prayer to Be Ready

Lord,
we must prepare for your return
to be counted among those
who have stood faithfully with you
to be here to witness your glory in full

the world fills the space around us
finds its way into our homes,
minds, hearts and souls

we become lost,
swept away with the rest of humanity

your word does not come back void
every day,
this world rushes to its conclusion
your prophecy moving ever closer to completion

all things must pass and the end is not yet
your inspired words come to fruition every day
with nation against nation,
famine and pestilence

we must live as if the world,
our world,
will end tomorrow
as you have spoken since time beginning

Modern Catholic Prayers

Jose Antonio Ponce

you have given humanity fair warning

your compassion is bestowed upon those who heed your word
those who live their lives in your mercy

Lord, bring us closer to you every day
fill us with the need to study your word to its completion
to understand the true meaning of your justice

give us the grace to be part of your plan
to lead others safely out of destruction
each day brings you closer
let each day bring us ever closer to you
bestow on us redemption

so that by your everlasting love
we may stand at your right hand
and worship in your presence forever

amen

A joyful heart is the health of the body, but a depressed spirit dries up the bones.-Proverbs 17:22

Prayer for a Joyful Heart

I know when my soul sings
when it is full of joy
and grace

but there are times when I am sick
lost in the world
scrabbling for something else
money, love, attention

joy leaves me
pushed out by the world

I become depressed
sick, lost,
abandoned
and begin to feel tired,
lost,
lonely, powerless

Lord, give to me the reasoning
to understand that your grace and joy
your presence
rescues my spirit

grant me peace and the understanding
that nothing in the world can satisfy my soul
like your love

Modern Catholic Prayers

Jose Antonio Ponce

help me to understand that there is no treasure
but you
that all wealth comes from you
and that in joy
is the secret to all that I desire

help me to bring your joy to others
so that we may all share in the wealth of your love
and bask in the radiance
of your grace

amen

Do not wear yourself out to gain wealth, cease to be worried about it; When your glance flits to it, it is gone! For assuredly it grows wings, like the eagle that flies toward heaven-Proverbs 23:4-5.

Prayer for a Modest Life

we rule the world around us
creating comfort wherever we go
raising the need for more
and more
and more

we try to maintain what we cannot hope to achieve
through possessions
pressured by the world around us
to live beyond our means

we hope to hold poverty at bay
with hardware
and lose sight of the need for spiritual riches

wealth is a weed
growing around our soul
and must be plucked away daily

Lord,
should we become so fortunate as to receive the
blessing of prosperity
create in us generous hearts
giving away all that we do not need

Modern Catholic Prayers

Jose Antonio Ponce

maintaining our lives
at a modest standard

help us to resist the temptation
of gaudy possessions

keep us from being owned by them
remind us that we need only
what is necessary to live
and to care for those whom we love

help us to live a life nearer to poverty than wealth
proving that your love
is a value beyond all riches

amen

I will be a father to him, and he shall be a son to me. If he does wrong, I will reprove him with a human rod and with human punishments 2 Samuel 7:14

The Step-Parent's Prayer

we have assembled this family
from bits of other families
sometimes from broken homes
sometimes from loss

we do our best to build a home
often asking children to accept us,
to divide their affection
between what they have always known
and what we are asking them to accept

newfound love
often excludes these children
pushes them away

Jesus, help each to remember
that you are the child of a step-parent

that blessed Joseph
gave up his whole life to care for you
and remained faithful
training you in the ways of the world
teaching you the value of humanity

Joseph, accepting his wife and her child
despite his concerns

protecting both from harm
earning a living
and never abandoning his responsibilities

Lord, give each the courage,
the patience
and the love and strength
to be a true parent to their children

show them your love, Father
through their actions
so that they may know you
and your boundless love and mercy

amen

Jose Antonio Ponce

Do not hate hard work; work was assigned by God.
Sirach 7:15

Prayer to be a Good Worker

Lord, we were meant to toil
without hard work,
we cannot appreciate a good life
without effort,
there is no reward

like the rain that falls from heaven
providing sustenance to all things
work provides a means to care for ourselves
and others

laziness breeds contempt for the world
jealousy and envy

let us give our best
to those who employ us

in public service grant us wisdom
empathy,
compassion

in our own efforts
bless us with honesty,
integrity
and a willingness to serve those gracious enough
to honor us with their trust
give us strength to carry the heavy load,

endurance to work a full day
and a willingness to do the best job that we can

an example to all
of the glory of your creation

amen

A worker's wage is credited not as a gift, but as something due.-Romans 4:4

Prayer of the Unemployed

I am without work
unable to care for my loved ones
unable to adequately do service to your name

Lord, help me to find the path
you have set for me
finding honest work in your world

your wisdom in designing for me
a life that will glorify your name
will provide me all that I need
to care for those around me

I seek only to do your will, oh Lord
to use the gifts that you have bestowed upon me
to their fullest potential

any skill or knowledge I possess
comes directly from you
through the parents,
teachers, and mentors
you have set before me

let not those gifts become idle
keep me on the course set for me
before I was created in the womb

remind me of your compassion for those enslaved,
impoverished and imprisoned by debt

when employment finds me
let me not forget those less fortunate

spur me into action to hire those
who have suffered from worry
and prompt me to provide them
with the comfort and security
of work that leads them to
your true purpose for their life

amen

Modern Catholic Prayers

Jose Antonio Ponce

I sought the Lord and he answered me and delivered me from all my fears.- Psalm 34:5

Prayer for Deliverance from Fear

this world is ruled by fear.
fear of rejection,
fear of poverty,
fear of anonymity.
the list is endless.

it drives the thief and the terrorist,
the politician and the pornographer,
the abuser and the addict.

fear thrusts us daily
into the world
with the hope that our actions
will bring relief.

we fear invalidity.
we fear isolation.
we fear persecution.

the devil, architect of fear,
sows seeds of doubt
creates division from fear
pits us against one another
to keep us always uncertain of your love.

the fear of war drives us to pursue war.

fear of loneliness foreshadows promiscuity.
our infirmities breed vanity.

you, Lord, have conquered fear
overcoming your own doubts in the garden
and sacrificing yourself
defeating death on the cross of salvation

have we forgotten your sacrifice?

want seeks immediate satisfaction.
pain solicits artificial relief.
persecution demands retribution.

if we are to remember you
in your glory
we must remember your courage

if death is defeated,
what is there to fear?

Lord, bless us with a portion of your courage.
drive the devil's fear from our pleading hearts
give us the strength to overcome fear,
to understand that nothing is impossible with you.

amen

To satisfy the one who recruited him, a soldier does not become entangled in the business affairs of life. 2 Timothy 2:4

A Soldier's Prayer

I am far from home, Lord
called by grace and duty
standing with my brothers and sisters
against an enemy I do not know

I seldom understand the reasons
for the madness that surrounds me
the terror,
the loss,
the twisted nature
that is war

I have witnessed horrors
no one should see,
done things that are unholy, but necessary
I have watched terrified children
become hardened soldiers

yet, I believe in what I am doing
without someone to defend them
these people would perish
at the hands of zealots

men who believe that they are god
or speak for god

Jose Antonio Ponce

men who punish as they believe
a ruthless god would punish

with cruelty and violence
without mercy or equity
without regard for truth

it is our task as soldiers
to protect these innocents
to give them a choice
other than death or insanity
to keep them safe
to make them whole again

it is a soldier's misfortune
to share in their suffering

they have lost family
we have lost brothers
all have lost innocence

oh, Lord, grant me empathy
for those who suffer
and compassion
for the victims of war

please give me the wisdom
to recognize my enemy
and to act justly toward him
to quell the anger in me for my loss

help me to remember that the rules of war

are the path to lasting peace

finally, grant me the forgiveness
that brings a peaceful heart
a quiet mind
and a soul
filled with your grace

amen

We do not want you to be unaware, brothers, of the affliction that came to us in the province of Asia; we were utterly weighed down beyond our strength, so that we despaired even of life. Indeed, we had accepted within ourselves the sentence of death, that we might trust not in ourselves but in God who raises the dead. He rescued us from such great danger of death, and he will continue to rescue us.- 2 Corinthians 1:8-10

Prayer of Soldiers Suffering from Post-Traumatic Stress

we are soldiers, Lord
survivors of war
once surrounded daily by death and violence
submerged in anger and hatred
running always toward danger
for the sake of our brothers and sisters
known and unknown
living in hostility

for months we stood on the edge of life
watching this one or that one die
by the most horrible means
while survivors
were scarred beyond recognition

now home
returned to our families
damaged,

nearly destroyed
unable to cope with the silence
unwilling to let go of the insanity of war

only the soldier understands us
and so many soldiers are lost
sometimes defined by the violence
guilty of the crime of survival
haunted by the memories of destruction

each volunteered to defend those oppressed by evil
just in our cause
but so consumed were we by war
that we cannot,
will not,
end the fight

you, Lord, know our pain
you, who watched over us
you, who we cried out to for safety,
whom we questioned
asking why we were chosen for this task

please, Lord,
give us the peace that we seek
ease the pain of memory
make our brothers and sisters whole again
if not in body, then in mind and spirit

give those around us an understanding heart
and the patience to help us heal

Jose Antonio Ponce

Lord,
hold the soldier close to you
comfort us,
calm us
help us to return to the sanity of home
and country

use the soldier as an example
as to why we should study war no more

amen

Modern Catholic Prayers

Jose Antonio Ponce

But now, thus says the Lord, who created you, Jacob, and formed you, Israel: Do not fear, for I have redeemed you; I have called you by name: you are mine. When you pass through waters, I will be with you; through rivers, you shall not be swept away. When you walk through fire, you shall not be burned, nor will flames consume you. - Isaiah 43:1-2

Prayer for Redemption from Agoraphobia

I am trapped, Lord
afraid of so many things
doomed to live in a world that I see as a constant threat

I am frightened
of what may happen
my mind races
with the possibilities
of the misfortune that awaits me

when I am out in public
every face seems menacing
every event promises peril

my heart beats
nearly uncontrollably
and I find it hard to catch my breath

there is no reason for this fear
no logical pretense for my apprehension
my world is limited to the space that I control
where everything is familiar to me

I know that your world is beautiful
miraculous
I have seen your power,
your beauty,
your magnificence
in so many things

yet, when I am among your creation
it brings only dread

help me, Lord, to overcome my fear
help me to trust
to find comfort
and acceptance
of the world around me

allow me the time to overcome my apprehension
bring me understanding from my friends,
my family
and, most of all, strangers

allow me the time to ease comfortably,
step by step,
into the world

give me the courage to step outside
to greet people with trust
to see the world as a gift
rather than a threat
to understand that the things in this life that are
menacing
are not from your divine hand

Modern Catholic Prayers

Jose Antonio Ponce

but the injustice of man
against man
and not directed at me

and when I find peace
it will be to your greater glory

amen

Limit the time you spend among the stupid, but frequent the company of the thoughtful. Sirach 27:12

Prayer to Make Wise Choices

Lord,
I am not the wisest person
by any measure
I find myself in situations
where I know I should not be

I have found temperance in maturity
and prudence in my daily affairs
but I am often caught up in the world

tempted and torn
easily steered toward destruction

I think to myself
"what harm could come?"
believing that I can return to my past

that my age
will keep me from falling from grace
I have come too close too many times

Lord,
give me the strength to make good choices
in my relationships,
in my work,
in my leisure
always remind me that only one sin

is still sin
and that the path to destruction
is but a single step
in the wrong direction

amen

Then he said to the crowd, "Take care to guard against all greed, for though one may be rich, one's life does not consist of possessions."-Luke 12:15

Prayer for a Satisfied Mind

I have spent my life chasing things
things that bring me momentary pleasure
things that do not edify

never did I once believe
that who I am,
what I am
was enough

I ran away from God's purpose
trying to find my worth
in the things that the world
taught me I should value
youth, beauty,
money, influence

only now do I understand
that God has created me
for a purpose

Lord, help me to remember
that I am here to reflect your glory
to be what you have created me to be

only you can take this broken-down vessel

this unwanted thing
and shining through me
bring to the world something beautiful

use me Lord
for your purpose
remove my conceit
my fear
my uncertainty

amen

For godly sorrow produces a salutary repentance without regret, but worldly sorrow produces death.-2 Corinthians 7:10

Prayer for Relief from Regret

Lord,
you have watched my life unfold
given me opportunity
and free will

in my life I have made mistakes
willfully disobeyed you
acted selfishly,
foolishly,
maliciously

harmed others through my own misconduct
at times, turned away from justice

after all these years
through the lens of regret
I clearly see the damage I have done
destruction I cannot reverse
for others or for myself

there are two kinds of regret
the regret of self
and the regret for the pain caused to others

please help me to overcome this regret
with charitable action

Modern Catholic Prayers

by revealing the damage done
so that my mistakes may not be repeated

ease this pain in my heart
the pain of failure
the pain of loss

give me the strength to move forward
and make myself worthy of your kingdom
so that I may reveal your glory
through kindness, justice and mercy
for all of my brothers and sisters

amen

Because of the abundance of the revelations.
Therefore, that I might not become too elated, a thorn in the flesh was given to me, an angel of Satan, to beat me, to keep me from being too elated. 2 Corinthians. 12:7

Prayer for Relief from Physical Affliction

Lord,
I am afflicted
tormented for so long

I have turned to every resource,
sought your wisdom,
prayed unceasingly
and yet my prayers go unanswered

the world revolves around me
perfect,
blissfully normal
while I carry on with this curse,
this leprosy that sets me apart

I am so alone
even among those who share my infirmity
I am, at best,
unseen
at worst ridiculed for what I am

through no fault of my own I suffer
sometimes doubting your grace and mercy
Lord, I feel cursed

Jose Antonio Ponce

help me to understand
and to face courageously
this disfigurement

give me the patience to endure
the grace to bless you
and give glory to your name
in the face of adversity

amen

Jose Antonio Ponce

Every day sorrow and grief are their occupation; even at night their hearts are not at rest. This also is vanity.
-Ecclesiastes 2:23

Prayer for Relief from Worry

each day I am anxious about the next
I sleep fitfully
afraid that I may not survive the morning's trials.

I am apprehensive about my job
fearful that I am not up to the task
certain that I can be replaced at any moment

I never seem to get ahead
of my duties,
my obligations,
my addictions

I am concerned about my physical health,
my spiritual well-being,
my social standing
and how I fit into the world

my life is constant worry

when I find respite in you, my God
in prayer and communication
the world pulls me back to itself
reminding me that I am not enough

Jose Antonio Ponce

Lord, please help me to remember
that your courage is always with me
that you too were abandoned
refused

you worried, doubted
but in the end
put aside your fears
stepped forward and put all fear to death

your courage
led to salvation

help me to remember
that this burden of doubt
are the remnants of sin
the remainder of the past
that this panic and can be abolished
though prayer and obedience
and faith

your burden should not go unrecognized
your sacrifice unacknowledged
you gave of yourself
so that we might live in peace

amen

Modern Catholic Prayers

Jose Antonio Ponce

In the same way, the Spirit too comes to the aid of our weakness; for we do not know how to pray as we ought, but the Spirit itself intercedes with inexpressible groanings. And the one who searches hearts knows what is the intention of the Spirit, because it intercedes for the holy ones according to God's will. God's Indomitable Love in Christ. We know that all things work for good for those who love God, who are called according to his purpose. - Romans 8:26-28

Prayers of Intercession and Petition

Prayer for the Community
Prayer in Defense of the Unborn
Prayer for Those Caring for an Aging Parent
Prayer for the Dying
Prayer for the Victims of Suicide
Prayer for Prisoners
Prayer for Immigrants
Prayer for Those in Poverty
Prayer for the Indigent
Prayer for Those in Cults
Prayer for Victims of Sexual Assault
Prayer for Pornographers
Prayer for the Victims of Violence
Prayer for the Poor Shepard

Two are better than one: They get a good wage for their toil. If the one falls, the other will help the fallen one. But woe to the solitary person! If that one should fall, there is no other to help. So also, if two sleep together, they keep each other warm. How can one alone keep warm? Where one alone may be overcome, two together can resist. A three-ply cord is not easily broken. - Ecclesiastes 4:9-12

Prayer for the Community

oh Lord
bless those in my life
who keep me whole

bless my wife for her patience, love and understanding

bless my mother for her age and wisdom

bless my father for his hard work and sacrifice

bless my siblings for their difference and guidance

bless my friends for their companionship, laughter and loyalty

bless my son for his strength and his challenges

bless my daughter for her beauty and fidelity

bless my neighbors for their watchful eye

bless my employer for my opportunities

bless my worship leaders for their piety and humanity

bless my animal friends for their devotion and unconditional love

amen

Your eyes saw me unformed; in your book all are written down; my days were shaped, before one came to be. - Psalm 139:16

Prayer in Defense of the Unborn

we have fallen away from you, Lord
allowing our passions to rule us
and letting the innocent pay for our mistakes

we have taught our children
that their mistakes can be erased
without consequence

have lied to them
about the aftermath
of such selfishness

bring us back, God
to the place where life is precious
where children are cherished
and not an inconvenience
or an uncomfortable situation

spur us to defend these most innocent of souls
with prayer and action
for prayer is the most powerful tool
and faith the catalyst for action

if we are to save ourselves
we must save our children first

bring us out of our ignorance
out of our selfishness
out of our fear of the world
so that the souls that bless creation
may first live among us
and give glory to your name

amen

Jose Antonio Ponce

My son, be steadfast in honoring your father; do not grieve him as long as he lives. Even if his mind fails, be considerate of him; do not revile him because you are in your prime. Kindness to a father will not be forgotten; it will serve as a sin offering, it will take lasting root. In time of trouble it will be recalled to your advantage, like warmth upon frost it will melt away your sins.-Sirach 3:12-15

Prayer for Those Caring for an Aging Parent

Father,
our parents gave selflessly
throughout our lives
from childhood through maturity
and beyond

please give us the courage and compassion
to care for our fathers and mothers
in the way they have cared for us

our parents were there
to pick us up when we fell
shared our joys
held and comforted us through our sorrows and disappointments

we need to be there
to care for them as their health fails
as their memories abandon them

give us the patience

to hold them up
to listen as they tell their stories
to care for their need

give us strength and courage
to be their refuge
in old age

amen

So, we are always courageous, although we know that while we are at home in the body we are away from the Lord, for we walk by faith, not by sight. Yet we are courageous, and we would rather leave the body and go home to the Lord. -2 Corinthians. 5:6-8

Prayer for the Dying

Lord,
we pray for those who are right now
breathing their last.

how lonely they must be

some, uncertain,
some, repentant
many in doubt
but all must surely be in fear

even with knowledge of your grace,
your compassion,
your love
all must wonder
"Did I do enough?"
"Have I wasted this gift?"
"Should I be punished?"

Lord, ease the pain of those who suffer through death
give time to those that seek repentance
surround those who have lingered with friends and family

give your greatest reward to those who have toiled
without hope
and comfort to those who have suffered the most

balance justice and compassion
and condemn no one for their crimes
rather, extend your hand
give each understanding
and peace from the evil
that has sought to torment them

in their final moments
allow them to understand
your love

amen

Jose Antonio Ponce

I give them eternal life, and they shall never perish. No one can take them out of my hand.- John 10:28

Prayer for the Victims of Suicide

oh my God
they have taken their own life

overwhelmed by despair and fear,
depression
or some other demon
they have given away
your precious gift

all of their promise is gone
and left behind
are those who grieve
at what can never be

Lord,
let not your word return void

your mercy transcends death
is beyond time

embrace these lost ones
bring them into your presence
and comfort them

give each one the peace
they could not find here

Jose Antonio Ponce

accept them as your children
broken though they may be
you will restore them to your glory

may they live in peace
in your kingdom
forever and ever

amen

Be mindful of prisoners as if sharing their imprisonment, and of the ill-treated as of yourselves, for you also are in the body.-Hebrews 13:3

Prayer for Prisoners

many languish, incarcerated
because of poor choices
or through no fault of their own

Lord,
remember those imprisoned
for just or unjust purposes
give them the strength to persevere
in a world filled with despair

give us compassion for their plight
and help us to remember them
and their families daily in prayer

keep us from condemnation
give us a fraction of the patience and understanding
that you have for the prisoner
for these lives interrupted
by sin or circumstance

spur us to action for their sake
let your love be reflected in us

let us not abandon those in prison
for each life has value
each soul is offered redemption

no matter the sin

give all a complete understanding
of your justice
and temper it with mercy

help us to fight for those
unfairly incarcerated
and give us pity for those justly condemned

give each a measure of your mercy
and an understanding that although condemned
we are redeemed by your love
your sacrifice

amen

Who executes justice for the orphan and the widow, and loves the resident alien, giving them food and clothing, so you too should love the resident alien, for that is what you were in the land of Egypt.- Deuteronomy 10:18-19

Prayer for Immigrants

my God,

this world of immigrants
seeking only a better life
come and go
from almost every place on earth

we sometimes see the immigrant as intruder, interloper
but they are us

we were once invaders
marauders
looked upon as pariahs

remind us that we were once aliens
persecuted for our color
our language
our beliefs

help us welcome the immigrant
granting asylum to the oppressed
offering protection to the persecuted
sharing our abundance
and granting opportunity

Jose Antonio Ponce

for each has value
each contributes
let us embrace all they have to offer
all that they are

emboldened by compassion
make us stronger as a nation
for we are all strangers here
and our true kingdom is heaven

amen

When one of your kindred is reduced to poverty and becomes indebted to you, you shall support that person like a resident alien; let your kindred live with you.-Leviticus 25:35

Prayer for Those in Poverty

Lord,
we have life so abundantly
and yet, let our neighbors live in poverty

often through no fault of their own
they live without what we take for granted
in constant fear of loss
of their meager possessions

there are those who have less everyday
because of our greed
because of our need
because of our want

fill us with compassion
for our impoverished brothers and sisters

spur us to action to share from our abundance
let us to deny ourselves
putting aside that
which would be wasted on mere possessions
and giving it to the poor

help us to raise our brothers and sisters up
to give graciously

Jose Antonio Ponce

and generously
to those in genuine need
so that the cycle of poverty
will cease to exist

remind us to act with charity
for your greater glory
giving in secret
and with all humility

amen

Jesus answered him, "Foxes have dens and birds of the sky have nests, but the Son of Man has nowhere to rest his head." Matthew 8:20

Prayer for the Indigent

we see them everywhere
every street corner
hosts at least one person
every bridge, a makeshift shelter

they carry their possessions
an odd collection of necessities
and small luxuries

meals are taken with strangers
they are dogged by violence
and resentment from others
who believe that they should disappear
that they are a blight

they beg for change
holding their signs
proclaiming their misfortune
"wounded vet"
"single mother"
"out of luck"

Lord,
give us compassion
for the indigent
those with no home

Jose Antonio Ponce

and little hope

let us give responsibly
help us make the change in our communities
that will eliminate their need
and bring peace and security
to their world

amen

Jose Antonio Ponce

I urge you, brothers, to watch out for those who create dissensions and obstacles, in opposition to the teaching that you learned; avoid them. For such people do not serve our Lord Christ but their own appetites, and by fair and flattering speech they deceive the hearts of the innocent. - Romans 16:17-18

Prayer for Those in Cults

many have been swallowed up
taken away from your redemption
by those with honeyed promises
often twisting your words

the innocent, the lost
the abused, lonely and preyed upon
hear this lyric and find false comfort,
short lived companionship and empathy

many offer wealth, success, self-determination
but bring only shame,
death and destruction

once they realize that they have been duped
these children are often unable to escape
held ransom by their secrets

your word, however, Lord, is truth
sharper than any sword
it can cut through the lies
bring comfort without condemnation

Modern Catholic Prayers

Jose Antonio Ponce

building up instead of tearing down

your word is all there is
living, breathing
a light for the world
truthful, powerful
and everlasting

bring your word
to those deceived
return them to a state of grace
free them from the furor
that controls and consumes them
to your greater glory

amen

Again, I saw all the oppressions that take place under the sun: the tears of the victims with none to comfort them! From the hand of their oppressors comes violence, and there is none to comfort them!
Ecclesiastes 4:1

Prayer for the Victims of Sexual Assault

Father,
their innocence has been stolen from them
any vision of love,
of tenderness or intimacy
has been destroyed
and they now live in fear

someone with more authority,
more power
has used them
and then tossed them away
their ability to trust, destroyed
they have been forced to trade themselves
for money
or security
or safety

send someone, Lord
to give them comfort
to ease their pain

they are not at fault
only victims of the cruelest evil
that destroys and leaves no physical scar

no way to see the damage done
we are a nation that glorifies sex
yet abhors sex crime
never making the connection

guide us, Father
into the light of pure love
where we care for one another
administer to each other's needs
and turn away from this evil

amen

Avoid immorality. Every other sin a person commits is outside the body, but the immoral person sins against his own body. Do you not know that your body is a temple of the holy Spirit within you, whom you have from God, and that you are not your own? For you have been purchased at a price. Therefore, glorify God in your body. 1 Corinthians 6:18-20

Prayer for Pornographers

Lord,
have mercy on those caught in the grip
of the sexual immorality
of pornography
especially those who produce these materials

guide them to a safer place
where they understand the harm done
by the evil there

lead them to an understanding of sex
as an expression of human love
rather than a simple means of pleasure

pornography destroys the soul
and the souls of those around them
the only thing in this world
corrupt by itself

offer your forgiveness,
your compassion,

your love

this sin as with all others
was purchased for their salvation
by your blood

the value of their lives
is more than the sum of their bodies
for each one holds
a soul worthy of heaven

turn each repentant voice
into a voice against this evil
and a new member of the chorus
that sings of your glory

amen

Jose Antonio Ponce

From extortion and violence he redeems them, for precious is their blood in his sight.- Psalm 72:14

Prayer for the Victims of Violence

there is brutality all around
there are those who would take from others
all they have earned
all they cherish
even, their very lives

beyond the act of violence
families are destroyed
communities upended
futures dismantled

greed, pride, jealousy
are the catalysts
for such destruction

Lord,
there is no understanding such devastation
and forgiveness is hard to find
so much has been taken away

give those who have suffered from violence
the strength to continue

let your courage and constancy
lift them up beyond fear,
beyond vengeance

Jose Antonio Ponce

let justice be their balm
forgiveness their healing
memory their comfort

for in you every wound is healed

amen

Woe to the shepherds who destroy and scatter the flock of my pasture.- Jeremiah 3:1-3

Prayer for the Poor Shepherd

Lord,
there are those of your ministry
who have forgotten their vows
or have traded their faith
for earthly treasures

others have succumbed
to temptations of the flesh
or the sin of pride

unable to lead through faith
they often become arrogant,
hard hearted
and judgmental
demanding respect
where none has been earned

Lord, help these men
who once believed in your word

bring them to justice if need be
return them to the faith
help them to remember
the core of their faith

do not abandon them to the world
rather renew them

Modern Catholic Prayers

Jose Antonio Ponce

forgive them
and bring them home

amen

Modern Catholic Prayers

Jose Antonio Ponce

Afterword

I began writing prayers nearly 10 years ago and somewhere along the line, decided to collect them in a book.

Each time I picked up the project, I was reminded of my arrogance. How could I believe that I had words sufficient for prayer? In my life, I have succumbed to every addiction, every sin. What could God possibly want with someone like me? What makes me think that God even listens to me?

In my teens, I walked away from the Catholic church because I wanted to live my life without consequence. If I prayed, I found I was just repeating words, distracted, thinking about everything except God. There was no praise, no thanks, no repentance. My prayer became repetitive, a mantra, a meditative drone.

Still, Christ was near me, in the lives of people doing good works in the community, those people helping others the world had forgotten. Oft times, these people were not Catholic or even Christian. They were just good people.

The things I learned about God in parochial school was also there, nagging me, telling me that I was taking a wrong turn or making a poor choice. As I grew older, I realized that the Catholic church, any church, is only as strong as the flawed people who are in control and that only God could make things right.

I began to understand that anyone could be forgiven. Even me. I knew in my heart that God believed in me even when I turned away from Him, that His mercy was endless. As a child, I had felt something during the mass, during the rosary. Later, during those desperate times when I was in private prayer begging for answers, I felt He was there with me.

Each night I pray the prayers I learned in Catholic school; the Our Father, the Hail Mary, the Doxology and a couple of prayers that I don't even know the names for.

I pray for the dead and for my family. I might choose one specific thing to pray on every night. It might be something that I heard in the news earlier in the day; a shooting, some natural disaster, a political situation or the for the souls of people lost in some man-made tragedy.

Often, I pray for people who are like me, for people who suffer from the same temptations, the same failings or for relief from the same economic and health worries that I deal with in my daily life. I attend mass every Sunday, but now the traditional prayers have a new importance to me.

Nothing can compare with divinely inspired prayers like the prayer of St. Francis of Assisi or the Psalms of David. These ancient prayers continue to speak to those things that are happening in my life and in the lives of others.

Jose Antonio Ponce

I struggle every day with the world, my pride and my weakness when it comes to putting myself first. When I pray from my heart, asking for God's blessing, for courage and for strength not just for myself, but for others as well, I realize that there are those who need God's help as much as I do, those who want to return to God, but, like me, can't imagine God wanting to take them back because of their sin.

I still worry about money and my family and friends and I still succumb to sin, but a friend of mine reminded me that God is in control, that nothing happens that he doesn't know about. I am here because God wants me here.

These tiny prayers I have put down here are merely my way of asking God's help for things that have burdened and confused the world. My hope is that others will find a connection with God through them.

I want to thank my pastor and friend the Reverend Monsignor Douglas Raun for reviewing each of the prayers for any inaccuracies or theological conflicts. Thanks also to my writing partner, Elizabeth Gabel for her honest insight into many of the things I do

Finally, thanks to my wife Kathy who has chosen a life of near poverty to allow me to write what I think might make a difference in someone's life.

Jose Antonio Ponce-November, 2021

The Lord never tires of forgiving us, never! We are the ones who get tired of asking forgiveness. Let us ask for the grace to never tire of asking forgiveness, because He never tires of forgiving us. Let us ask for this grace." Pope Francis

Modern Catholic Prayers

Jose Antonio Ponce

Other books by Jose Antonio Ponce

Fiction
Killing Coyote (a novel)

Short Stories and Essays
work@home
Lunch Hour

Proverbs
From Father to Son

Poetry
53-Coming of Age in the 70's

Learn more about the author at *joseantonioponce.com*

www.ingramcontent.com/pod-product-compliance
Lightning Source LLC
Chambersburg PA
CBHW060603080526
44585CB00013B/673